HOW TO CREATE A KICK-A** BLOG:
The Ultimate step-by-step Guide for Beginner Bloggers

SARAH LEIGH

ISBN: 978-17-17801-73-9

DEDICATION

To all the new bloggers entering the blogosphere.
May the power of the blog be with you!

CONTENTS

LETTER FROM THE AUTHOR

The fact that you are reading this book shows me that you really *are* serious about blogging! That's great! This book explains everything that newbies to the Blogosphere need to know in order to set up your own kick-ass blog! When I first thought about blogging as more than just a hobby, I did a little bit (ok, a LOT) of research into *what* I actually needed to do in order to create a blog. Since I "launched" my blog ('Life It Or Not') in May 2018, I have learnt so much and come so far in such a short amount of time that I feel I should tell other beginner bloggers how to do it too!

As you may have already noticed, there are tons of awesome books, info graphics and posts that tell you "a lot about a little", i.e., they focus on one or two of the main parts of blogging. Some might focus on the setting up of WordPress, some on SEO, some on content etc. Don't get me wrong, those are mostly great reads, but I have only come across a small handful that are about the whole shebang…how to create a blog – everything you need to know!

PROLOGUE

What is so special about this book?

This book is unlike other books that are out there because it is not going to push or pull you in one direction or another. Everything in this book is from a fresh perspective and an up-to-date experience on the Blogging World. It is also one of the only "shorter-length" blogging books out there that gives a simple, but informative explanation of all the steps you need to take in order to create, launch, promote, maintain *and* monetise your own blog.

This book will provide you with the basic knowledge and understanding (and an impartial view) on things like growing a network, finding your niche, self-hosted vs. free platforms, affiliate links and much, much more. It will give you the ability to choose for yourself *what* you want to do and *how* you want to do it – rather than me pushing my own views and opinions onto you.

Why did I start blogging?

Within three months of the birth of my lil' Squidge

(my daughter) in January 2017, she had been diagnosed with partial deafness and was given a hearing aid. At the same time, I was going through a Cervical Cancer Scare, I was diagnosed with Dilated Cardiomyopathy and Heart Failure, and oh yes, can't forget the big one…my partner (Squidge's dad) then decided to leave us! What should have been an amazing family time of love and cheer and baby laughter, turned out to be a time of stress, worry, confusion, anger and sadness.

Of course though, my amazing Squidge and my family and friends were my light, keeping my head up and my mind in the right zone throughout it all – thanks my lovelies. As a release for all this stress, I started writing about Squidge's life and mine – in the form of a "personal online journal" kind of thing. One of my friends saw my ramblings and told me to start sharing my story and inspiring others. I never really saw myself as a Motivational Speaker type, so I thought I would start by just changing the direction of my blog and aiming my writings at other women and mums who might need a little push to get to where they want to be. The more I researched and met other people in the blogging industry, the more obsessed I became with blogging. I haven't stopped since!

iii

SARAH LEIGH

INTRODUCTION

What is a blog?

You have probably read hundreds of blogs without even realising it! Anytime you have read something online that seemed to be written in a more "conversational tone" than a formal one, it was more than likely a blog. Ever heard of "weblog"? Well, that's what a "blog" was originally called. Blog is just short for Weblog.

A weblog/blog is essentially an informal (often personal) website or webpage that is updated regularly. It shows posts in reverse chronological order, with the most recent posts displayed at the top of the page. A blog can be like a diary or journal that is founded, run and contributed to by just one or two people (the blogger or bloggers) or a way for someone to share their expertise or thoughts about a given subject. Businesses and big organisations are also now seeing the benefits of blogging and are employing people to actually run a full blog for their business.

That "subject" that I mentioned in the previous paragraph is called a "niche". All blogs fit into a niche – or even more than one (take Lifestyle bloggers, for example). This niche is normally either a topic that the author is passionate about, or a topic that can make them money. For example, most people want to know how to make money quick, so some bloggers write about just this – and they actually make money in the process because by following their own advice.

Why should you start a blog?

There are a multitude of reasons why you should start a blog. Obviously, the first reason being because you actually want to give it a go. Most people either start a blog in order to earn more money on the side or to share their opinions or life journeys with others, but once people start really listening to you and taking in your posts, you become an authority. When you can show that you really are an expert in your field – whether it be parenting, fashion, making money, cleaning or even making crafts, your readers will see you as someone to trust. They will refer back to your posts because they are drawn to your knowledge and writing and want to know more.

Blogging provides you with a platform on which you get an opportunity to meet likeminded people and even engage with leaders, other professionals and maybe even your own idols in your niche. Once you build an online relationship with these people, they might even start sharing your posts to their hundreds of thousands of followers and you will become known as someone who is on the same level as them.

Do you need to already be successful to start a blog?

Of course not. Since when do you have to be "successful" to share your own opinion and knowledge? In no way at all do you need to be famous, well known or even popular in your own area to start a blog! In fact, most blogs are started by "normal" people in their own home. Everybody has to start somewhere and almost all bloggers start from scratch.

The one thing that you DO need to start a blog, is at least a *good* knowledge and level of expertise in the thing you are blogging about. You can't pretend to teach others about something if you don't have the first clue about it yourself, and you definitely can't be using other bloggers posts as a basis for yours (although research for inspiration-sake is ok).

Is it easy?

At first, I honestly thought that blogging would just mean writing a new post and sharing it once a week and that would be it!

Haha! I couldn't have been more wrong!

Blogging requires determination, inspiration, consistency, time management and organisation skills, patience, resilience, integrity and *effort*...A lot of characteristic and personality words in there, I know, but I've probably missed lots out too! Realistically, if you actually want to get serious about your blog, you will not be able to do it as an "as and when" hobby. Although I initially started blogging as a way to document my heart health journey and my life as a single mum, once I realised how many different topics actually related to my life, I realised that this whole blogging malarkey was going to be a huge, time-consuming job! Good news though – It is *definitely* worth it!

My first month of blogging...

After two weeks of planning my blog out as a business, reading and learning, promoting, writing, drinking lots of (decaf) coffee (and a bit of wine) and lots of night-time playing around and editing of my website, I finally started to receive visitors. If I had not started to put the time into everything I needed to, I never would have got a single visitor to my blog! My numbers are growing quickly because of my consistency and dedication to my blog. In just my first month, my Pinterest views grew from 0 per day to over 5k per day. A few days after my 1-month "Blogiversary" (yes, I celebrated it!), it had reached 104k views.

My blog itself had grown from 0 views per day to between 200-400 per day. Staying on those numbers consistently, that would mean an average of over 8k website visits per month! Of course though...it was only my first month, so these numbers went up and down quite a bit at first.

2

YOUR BLOG DIRECTION

Focus on your "Aim", not your "Niche"

I'm going to start pretty controversially here...I hate the word "niche"! You will find many split opinions on this one all over the internet from various influential bloggers and newbies alike, but my *personal* opinion is that you don't need to spend ages stressing over whether you fit into a "niche" or even whether there is any point in actually starting a blog in the first place because there are already so many bloggers in your chosen niche! Instead, if you can pinpoint *WHAT* you actually want to achieve with your blog, you will find that your blog automatically just slips into a niche category.

My blog went through a few stages at first - from being for other single mum's to read about my life in general, to mums who suffer from Cardiomyopathy, to single mums only. When I stopped thinking about what I wanted to WRITE and started thinking about what I wanted to CHANGE, I finally found my niche/s: Parenting, Lifestyle and Personal Growth. I now write about my life in a way that can help and inspire others. Regardless of what people say about making money from your blog, think about how long you will be able to write about something that doesn't interest you, or that you are not passionate about?

☺ ACTIVITY 1:

Ask yourself the following questions and answer them in the spaces provided.

What interests you the most?

_____

_____

_____

What are you passionate about?

_____

_____

_____

What are you most proud of?

_____

_____

_____

What difficulties have you overcome?

_____

_____

_____

What do you want to change?

_____

_____

_____

What do you want to achieve through your blog?

_____

_____

_____

What are you good at?

_____

_____

_____

Which problems are you good at solving?

_____

_____

_____

Branding

Blog Name

I think it goes without saying that you want your blog name to stand out! It is also a very good idea to get your keyword/s in your blog name for the sake of Search Engine Optimisation (SEO). Because my blog name does not feature any of the keywords associated with my blog topic or niche (there's that word again!), I have battled with SEO to get it recognised by search engines etc.

I was pretty much set on 'Life It Or Not' from the start – the only thing that changed was that it was initially written with a hash tag (#LifeItOrNot). Believe it or not, that did not make for good social media and it also looked a bit weird on the logo. I changed it to Life It Or Not within just the first couple of weeks.

Tagline

Do you need a tagline? Maybe. Maybe not. It all depends on your blog name and logo / header. Does your blog name tell you exactly what your blog is about? If not, you probably need a tagline. The tagline is basically a short sentence (usually placed in your header, under your blog name), which describes your blog completely. 'Life It Or Not' is not a very specific blog name, so I added my tagline underneath my logo on the header. It now reads, "Empowering Women to Become Their Own Inspiration."

This draws the attention of my target audience (women) and tells them that I want to empower them to become inspired. This gives the impression of strength and belief in myself and creates a sense of trust from my readers.

Logo

My first ever logo was made on an online site and rather than paying for it (I clearly was not that serious at first), I actually took a screenshot of it...yes, I'm already embarrassed enough! I can feel your disgust! Of course, there were huge problems with doing this. The main issues were that a screenshot gets blurry when the size is adjusted and the background is not transparent (so you can only put your logo on a background colour that matches the actual background colour of the screenshot).

After looking around online, I came across the 'Wix Logo Creator'. For just under £10, I was able to download **eight** versions of my logo – black or monochrome on a white or transparent background, white writing on a black background, and other options like these. These images are also 'high-resolution', so they are able to stretch and be re-sized much more easily. They are also way more professional looking!

Style

Contrary to what people might think, branding is so much more than just your logo! It is the first thing that your readers notice before anything else – including your amazing content! Branding is the colours you use on your blog-site, the fonts you prefer, the layout, the types of pictures, and your "tone of voice". Is your writing voice sarcastic, serious, happy, informative etc.? It is also the delivery of advertising (do you sell by placing ads on main pages, or do you do it in links?).

Example from my own blog:

I use shades of pink, orange and grey in my branding. My font of choice is Lucida Sans (Sans fonts are used more in blogs because they apparently seem to be more trusting!), and I write with an informative, but supportive tone, which is (hopefully) easy for beginners and the everyday person to understand. I also prefer to deliver my advertising and affiliate links through in-text links, rather than through visible ads on my pages. I do, however, currently have a couple of AdSense ads dotted here and there for tiny bump of monetization (which I will discuss later in this book).

SMART blog goals

In my years as an educator, I have spent way too much time learning about, setting, teaching and delivering on SMART goals! When setting yourself a goal, it has to be specific.

There is no point in saying you just want to be a good blogger or you want to have a thousand readers a month. You have to set yourself specific goals – otherwise, how will you actually be able to measure your success?

☺ **ONGOING ACTIVITY:**

Every time you set yourself a goal, make sure you remember to work SMART!

Specific

What *exactly* is it that you want to achieve? Do you want to earn £100 a month from your blogging? Do you want to gain 50 subscribers in one month? Do you want to guest post on three different parenting blogs in three weeks? Think about *why* this goal is important to you and whom you might need to involve to make it a success (fellow bloggers, businesses, online apps etc.)

Measurable

How will you actually measure your progress towards your goal? How will you know when you have achieved it? Make this one motivating and meaningful – make your measure of your success something that will make you proud!

Achievable

Can you actually achieve this goal? Is it worth the effort and time you will put into it – do you even *have* that effort and time to do so in the first place? Don't make it too easy or it won't be worth it, but don't make it so hard that you will be upset if and when you don't manage to achieve it because you set the bar too high. Make sure YOU are the only person who can affect the outcome of this goal. Yes, you might need someone else's help to do it, but if that doesn't work, you should still be able to find a way around it. Just don't put all your eggs into someone else's spoon.

Relevant

Don't pick a goal like making 50 new subscribers if you already have 500 and it is growing steadily. Rather, pick a goal that is more relevant to you – relate it to where you are "lagging" (if anywhere) or to something that you really feel you want to improve or achieve. Is it the right time in your blog life to be making this goal? Or would it be best suited and more realistically achievable further down the line?

Timely

If you don't have a deadline, you are much less likely to achieve your goal. Working to a deadline keeps you on your toes and makes you feel 10x happier when you finally reach your goal after all of your hard work. You did it in the timeframe you gave yourself…go you!

Know your Target Audience

It might be hard to accept, but not everyone is going to love – or even care about what you write or sell! Before you start writing *anything,* you need to know **whom** you are actually writing for. If you try to appeal to everyone, it will appeal to no one. My wider target audience is women, aged 21-40 who want to be a better version of themselves.

The *even more* targeted version of this is: The single mum, aged 30ish, who is a stay-at-home mum, or works part-time and is all about the kid/s. She enjoys reading books/online blogs, cooking, music, travel and having fun. Her challenges are that although she enjoys doing all of those things, she is unable to actually do it all for some reason...this is where Life It Or Not comes in!

☺ ACTIVITY 2:

Try to actually *"picture"* your target
audience in your mind…
then answer the following questions.

How old are they?

_____

What are they like?
(Frugal, self-conscious, creative, active etc.)

_____

_____

_____

What industry do they work in *(if they work)*?

_____

What are their values and lifestyles?

_____

_____

_____

_____

What are their hobbies?

_____

_____

What are their pain points?
(The things that really bother them)

_____

_____

_____

What questions or challenges do they face?

_____

_____

_____

How can you help them to answer their questions and solve their problems?

3

CREATING YOUR WEBSITE

Free Vs. Self-Hosted Platforms

What is the difference between the publishing (website) platform, domain and host?? Simply put:

Publishing or Website Platform

The tool you use to actually design and create your website.

Domain: Your online address (www.yoursite.com)

Host: Your landlord.

Your domain cannot just hover around in online space. It needs to have a place to "live". Your host is the "area" in which your address (domain) will live. This is why you have to pay your host – it is your landlord.

Free

"Free" website creation platforms are great for beginners as they are so easy to use. The best thing about "free" platforms is that the setup, hosting, firewalling etc. is all already done for you, so you only have to concentrate on creating your content and making the site look appealing (amongst other things, obviously), while your host does all the nitty-gritty dirty work. Wix, Blogger, Weebly and many other blogging platforms are all classed as "free" websites, but in order to use the full features, you have to pay! You can't fully monetize most free blogs properly.

There are limits on which ads and how many ads can be displayed. Most free platforms actually add their own ads to your website that you can't remove unless you pay. This not only looks unprofessional, but it is also a huge pain for you! There are usually restrictions to the plugins, customization options and analytics available on free platforms, and some have a limited number of customization options and little to no plugins, even after paying for a full account. With "free" platforms, you have little to no authority over your own website (depending on which platform you use). The platform could just suspend – or even delete your account and website at any time, and you wouldn't have a say in the matter!

Nightmare!

You also do not own your domain name. It would look something like *username.wix.com/yoursitename* – NOT a good look! Although, like I said before, if you are happy to fork over some extra cash, you can get your own domain name extremely easily.

Self-hosted

Self-hosted platforms are also good for beginners as they can help you to develop your SEO, HTML and design skills, but they are quite a bit trickier to dive into! Self-hosted platforms are much more enticing for a HTML pro than a free (already hosted) platform. You will very rarely see someone who is skilled with computers, the Internet and HTML creating a website on Wix or Weebly. The best thing about self-hosted websites is that you own your domain and have full control over what happens to your account. You are also able to be much more creative (as you can use HTML to add things that you may not be able to find in plugins or widgets).

The downside of self-hosting is that, although the platform itself is free, you have to pay the host "rent" to keep your website there – which can cost a fair amount! You can decide to either pay monthly or do a one off payment to cover the whole year.

Why I made the move from "free" to self-hosted

In the beginning, I spent a lot of time...and I mean a LOT of time editing my Wix website to get it (almost) just how I wanted it. I had paid for the yearly subscription for my domain so that I wouldn't have to pay the slightly higher amount each month and was ready to rock the Wix World with my blog! Why did I choose Wix in the first place? Simple. I had used it before (for a music artist website and some other bits and bobs) and it did everything I needed it to then. I just didn't realise how much *extra* I would need for a blog!

When I chose to use Wix (already hosted) for my blog, I didn't know about the importance of

AdSense the need to **download a document** straight from a text link in a blog post or the need to put an **opt-in and advertisement boxes** in blog posts! With Wix, all of these things were either not possible, or were possible, but were not very reliable. I also didn't know how important it would be for an external email-marketing platform like **MailChimp** to be able to put an opt-in pop up box before allowing access to content upgrades. Whilst on Wix, I was unable to do most of the things that I wanted to do with my blog, so I knew I had to move to another platform. WordPress is the most-used self-hosted platform in the world!

I decided to use WordPress.org (self-hosted) rather than WordPress.com (hosted) because of the opportunities and freedom that I found I could have with the self-hosted platforms.

Karol K on Codeinwp.com states that these are the current WordPress statistics (correct as of May 2018):

- WordPress runs 30% of the entire Internet

- 17 posts are published every second on WordPress sites around the world

- The keyword "WordPress" gets googled around 2.8 million times every month

- WordPress.org has 50k+ plugins in its official directory

WARNING!!

I decided to move my domain from Wix to WordPress (via my new host, SiteGround) about 30 days after I purchased my domain name. What I DID NOT know was that you actually have to wait a whole 60 days after purchasing the domain name before you are allowed to transfer it to another host.

I designed my WordPress site in just under a week, transferred all of my posts etc. to my new site (as I only had a small number of posts, I just copied and pasted them) and re-uploaded the images. I then spent the next few days online talking with SiteGround reps trying to get my DNS pointing to my new host (a long process but it worked eventually). SiteGround reps were amazing!!

NOTE

DNS is Domain Name System/Servers. It is basically just a system that points your domain name to a new address (this was a good way to get my new site up and running before I was allowed to fully transfer my domain name over).

Hosts

As I mentioned before, your host is basically your landlord. If you have a problem with your pipes or your electricity, your landlord normally sorts this out. You pay your host "rent" to keep your website alive and running. If you have a bad landlord, you could be waiting ages, have to pay extra for a service to be done or it might never even get fixed. If you have a good landlord, life becomes a lot easier – and happier! Whatever you do, make sure your actually do some research into which host you want to use!

There are a multitude of different hosts out there, all claiming to be the best, but you really need to look deeper than just into what *they* say about themselves. Look at reviews, online videos, look at the support available and read comments about them online. The most popular hosts are Bluehost, SiteGround, HostGator and GoDaddy. I eventually chose SiteGround to be my host.

Why?

Well, the main reason was that the support available seemed to be the best at the time. They definitely lived up to their promise! I had never used a self-hosted platform before and if I'm completely honest, I was terrified that I would put loads of time and energy into my blog just for me to do something wrong that would mess it all up. I *needed* to know that there was a proper support system in place! That was my number one priority.

You will of course, have your own priority and will make your own decision based on what is most important to you when starting your blog. I was also drawn to SiteGround for other reasons. The uptime (percentage of time that the host server is actually working and available online) is 99%, the domain transfer process was simple and cheap and the registration services and extra costs were low.

Domain name

Your domain name is just as important as your blog name. It is your name, your address, your SEO kicker and your identity! Purchase your own domain name! If you build a website for free, you are more than likely going to be given a "sub-domain" which means that it won't be as simple and memorable as:

www.*yourblogname*.com

It is more likely to be something like :

www.websiteprovidersname/yourblogname.com

It just doesn't have that professional touch about it, does it? You must ensure that your domain name is simple and easy to remember and that it is very closely related to your blog or niche. If you can, try to make it as close to your actual blog name as possible. You don't want a blog name of "Life It Or Not" which has a domain of:

www.sarahsparenting.com

Choose the end of your domain wisely. .Com, .Org and .Net are all classed as "top-level domains" (TLD). They are the most-used domain extensions in the world and are unrestricted open domains. There used to be more of a meaning for each one, but these days they are not noted for such purposes, as pretty much anyone can choose to affix any extension to their domain. .Com is a commercial business, .Net is a network organisation and .org is a non-profit organisation. For SEO purposes, .Com is the best choice to go for, followed by .Org and then .Net

Pages

Home

Lets start with your Home page. You probably think that most people start on your blog from the Home page, right? Wrong! Most people who visit your blog will be going straight to one of your posts. If they like what they read, they will start having a peek around at other parts of your blog. Some people put their most recent posts on their homepage...don't do this! Although this is good for SEO purposes (keeping the content fresh and updated), it is NOT good for enticing new readers.

It is much better if you just include a couple of your best, most amazing eye-catching posts for your new readers to see how awesome you are! Did you know that 15 seconds is the average length of time that a visitor will spend on your website before they get bored and decide to leave. Your homepage should be neatly laid out and should clearly explain what you do or what services you offer to the reader.

Provide a *little bit* about your background and experience (not too much as you will have this all in your About Me section) and maybe even feature a testimonial or two if you have any. Some people even call their Home page 'Start' or 'Start Here' as it tells newbie visitors of the blog what they can expect from you and how you can benefit them. If you cannot make this clear from the get-go, why would they bother staying on your website? It's not like they're going to care enough to spend ages searching all over your website to find something that says what you actually provide.

About Me

I started my 'About Me' section all wrong! My first About Me page had huge paragraphs all about how my life started and what I went through before I started my blog. This is good in a way, because you want the readers to know why you are actually an expert in your area and why they should trust what you say, but don't go writing your entire life story. Although it is the About YOU page, try to think of it as an ABOUT MY BLOG page.

☺ **ACTIVITY 3:**

To help you start writing your 'About Me' section, draft your ideas here…

Why you started your blog

_____

_____

_____

What makes you an expert in this field?

_____

_____

_____

_____

If you are not an expert in your field, what is it about your experience that should make your reader trust what you have to say?

_____

_____

_____

What about your blog? What is it all about?

_____

_____

_____

_____

What can the reader expect to get from your website?

_____

_____

_____

_____

Don't Forget

Add your contact info at the bottom of the page – don't expect the reader to drag themself over to the Contact Page. It is much easier for them to just email you or use a contact form / social media links straight from the page they are reading.

Blog

This one is self-explanatory. You will need a page for your blog. However, there are many different ways that you can actually present your blog. Most layouts or themes offer a few options for display. These options normally include:

- Simple list of your most recent blog posts

- Short description of the post with a thumbnail image

- A larger (full width) image with a longer description

- Some offer the option to put the whole post on the page!

Categories

Where will your categories go? There are loads of options for how you will present your blog to your readers.

- Will you have just one page on your menu that says "Blog" and then a drop-down menu of your categories?

- Maybe you have no actual "Blog" page at all, and just have the individual categories lined up on your menu?

- Do you have enough posts to add sub-categories to your main categories? Will these be as drop-downs or not even on display?

NOTE

Remember: *If you have a lot of categories (I would say, more than 5), you might find it difficult and a bit cluttered to put all of them on the Main Menu.*

On Life It Or Not, my menu features the following pages: Home, About Me, Lifestyle, Personal Growth, Parenting, Blogging and Contact Me. I have added a sub-category of Cardiomyopathy into the Lifestyle main category. The main reason I did this is that Cardiomyopathy is a smaller niche that I target – so it doesn't have enough posts for me to want to give it it's own menu page. The second reason I did this is that my main menu would have seemed too crowded if I had added it as a main category.

Contact

It is crazy how many bloggers actually forget to put what they want to be contacted *about* on their Contact Page! If you were an advertising agent and you wanted to offer some sponsored posts or ad space to a blogger, but when you went onto their contact page, there was just a contact form, you wouldn't be very impressed. Make sure you have a couple of sections that actually explain what you offer to advertisers.

Do you also offer guest posts? Include this too. Some bloggers even create a separate page, just for PR and advertising! Do you actually want to have guest posts on your blog yet? If not, make a point of saying so – otherwise, you might end up with a ton of emails from other bloggers asking for or offering posts. The same goes for product reviews or sponsored posts. If you want advertisers and businesses to contact you about these sorts of things, you need to actually *tell them.* For example, you might want advertisers and businesses to contact you via email, but readers and other bloggers to contact you via the contact form. Make this clear on your Contact Page.

Legal stuff

Disclosures

If you are monetising your blog, you will definitely need one of these. See Chapter 5: Monetise your Blog.

Privacy Policy

You WILL need a Privacy Policy! A Privacy Policy is a legal statement or agreement where you disclose all of the ways in which you collect, use, disclose and manage / use a readers personal information. If you use Google Analytics, AdSense, affiliate links and any other systems that use any personal information, you need to legally let your readers know. This must be clear on your website –

too many bloggers add a little policy of a few sentences at the bottom of a page somewhere so that it doesn't affect the aesthetics of the website. I personally prefer to see one as it tells me that the website owner is more professional and transparent. Don't start panicking though, as with the Disclosure Statement, you can easily just Google for examples that you can then copy, paste and edit to suit your own use.

Sidebar Content

Your sidebar is the only part of your website (other than your header and menu) that is always on show. The sidebar is also a place to put information or links that you want your readers to have easy, quick access to. REMEMBER: The **Fold** is the section of your website that shows at the top of your page before you scroll. It is the one part of your website that is automatically seen by anyone and everyone who visits your site. For this reason, you should put everything that is most important – and most relevant at the top of your sidebar, in the **fold**.

A good sidebar will feature important widgets and information, which will benefit the reader and will NOT negatively affect their sessions on your blog. Think about what *you* would and would not like to see in a sidebar?

About me link

Your About Me page link should go at the top (or *very* near to the top) of the Sidebar! You want people to be able to find out about you and your blog easily. Although you may already have an About Me page link on your main menu, this is much easier to grab a readers attention, as it almost always has an image attached to it.

Social Network Links

These links are often attached to the About Me box. This does NOT mean that you shouldn't also put them further down in your sidebar too (just in case a reader scrolls without seeing the first ones). Pick the platforms you are most active on. You don't want a selection of 10 different social networking platform links to confuse your reader. Keep it simple and just use the ones that you use the most.

Subscribe box

Obviously! Not only will you need these somewhere in EVERY blog post (depending on the length of the post, I put one in the middle and one at the end of each post), but you will also need (at least) another nice obvious one on every page.

Ad for an eBook or eCourse

Are you selling or promoting a new eBook or eCourse? Pop that in your sidebar too! You might even have a free sample of the book or course linked to a subscription opt-in box.

Categories

If you don't have these on your menu or in a drop-down menu, you need to have them somewhere obvious that is easily accessible for your readers.

Ads

Ok, so you might not want to see ugly ads splattered all over a post you are reading, but one in the middle of a sidebar and another down the bottom is not going to heavily affect reader retention. Depending on the type of ad, you may even be able to customise the design of the ad to fit your branding (Google AdSense allows this).

Archives

This one, of course, depends on how long you have been blogging for. If you have published less that 20 blog posts, you probably don't need an Archives menu.

Popular posts

If your readers enjoyed reading the post that actually bought them to your blog in the first place, they may want to see other popular posts. This is a great space for you to promote your best work – and grow those view numbers and shares even more!

Plugins and HTML

When I was only using Wix, life was a lot easier…but a lot more boring!! Since I started using WordPress, I have (accidentally) started learning about HTML – Yay! There are so many plugins and customisation tools available online, it's *crazy*!

There are things to embed, plugins to add, CSS and HTML to edit (building blocks of your web page), short codes to input (little shortcuts to input plugins), pop-ups to link (like an opt-in box) and widgets to add. I love it!

Plugins

A plugin is a little piece of software that can add awesome features to your website. You download it or install and activate it to be able to use it. You can get some amazing plugins for free but *most* of the best ones are paid, or require payment to unlock the best features. The two plugins that I literally couldn't live without:

1. Akismet (anti-spam plugin)

2. Yoast SEO (the DON of plugins when it comes to SEO corrections)

Widgets

A widget is essentially a drag-and-drop tool with limited functionality for people who do not have HTML or CSS knowledge. A widget adds content and features to your website. Widgets are normally only used in the sidebar.

The three widgets that I will always have in my sidebar:

1. Social Icons (so they can follow me on my social media)

2. Subscribe Box

   3. About Me box (to link to my About Me page)

4

CREATIVE KILLER CONTENT

Build your mailing list

As a brand new blog, you won't start off with a huge following initially and may find it quite tricky and frustrating to get your subscriber email list growing – I know I did! I might have had over 100k Pinterest views in my first month, but I only had 4 subscribers…one of them was my mum! Through doing my research (I love researching!), I found that using a pop-up subscribe box can (apparently) boost your subscribers by 200%! So I started using one.

It was displaying extra-large on mobile devices, so I had to put a stop to using those until I figured out how to fix the issue. I realised I had to pay for it and at that time, I wasn't ready to invest even more money (silly me!). I still kept using the desktop pop-up though. This pop-up enticed another nine subscribers in two weeks. Although it might not sound like a lot, it was actually three-times as many subscribers as I got in the first month of my blog!

I also started to think about email opt-in incentives! This e-book right here is one of my email incentives. The way I see it is: I am spending a lot of time and effort in writing this e-book. As an opt-in incentive, I am offering one whole chapter of this book for free. All I ask for in return is their loyalty and email address so I can keep sharing awesome things with them.

There are plenty of things you can create as an opt-in incentive:

- Printables and Downloads

- eBooks

- Subscribers-only content

- Digital Workbooks

- Second half of a blog post (you can use something really cool called a "hidden content box" for this!)

- eCourses or Email Workshops (with downloadable worksheets and/or printables)

- Video / Audio downloads

- Random giveaway to a subscriber every month

- Downloadable cheat sheets

- Pinterest schedule template / planner

- Downloadable checklists

- Free preview of an eBook, eCourse or Workshop

- Content upgrades (discussed below)

Create plenty of content (posts)

Some people have launched their blog-sites when they only have about 5 "ok-ish" posts and then wonder why they are not getting any return visitors or subscribers (yep, I did this!) Have you ever clicked on a post that tickled your fancy and then gone to see the bloggers other posts, only to discover that they only have a couple – which are not even that good? I have! It is annoying because they want me to subscribe, but what am I subscribing to? So, obviously, I don't subscribe – or return to that blog.

If you don't have at least 15-20 original posts on your page, you will find it hard to draw people's attention in (unless you tell them that it is a new blog – which sometimes works in your favour, but mostly doesn't).

What is the ideal post layout?

Headline

You need a catchy headline with keywords in for SEO purposes (*more on this later*). Something that really draws the reader in – this is the first thing they will see after all! Some people have sub-headlines just to reiterate and make the main message even clearer.

Main image

Most good blogs have some kind of bright and clear image just underneath the headline (or even *as* the headline!) This makes the post brighter and friendlier to the eye.

Intro

Pretty obvious. You have to give the reader a quick idea of what it is that they are about to read. I have clicked on a few posts thinking it is about one thing but then they go on to talk about something I don't even care about.

Main Content

This is your bread and butter! The main thing your readers come to your blog for. You have to make your main content engaging and interesting to read. If it is just regurgitating affiliate links (*more on this later*) or writing in huge paragraphs, it won't give the feeling that it is tailored to your reader. Use short sentences (in fact, in Yoast's 'Readability' check, it suggests that a sentence of more than 20 words is too long!).

Linked very closely to what I mentioned in the Introduction section – if your content is not 100% related to your title, you will completely turn your readers off. For example, when I was first setting up my blog, I clicked on a post about 'Blogging for Success' (or something like that). When I clicked on it, the intro explained that the author would discuss how to SET UP a successful blog...so I continued to read. After a few paragraphs, it was clear that the author was only going to be talking about setting up a blog using WordPress. He gave a pretty good outline of how to create a WordPress blog. But, that was it really.

Now, this would be great for someone interested specifically in setting up WordPress, but the title and intro were misleading. I thought I would be reading about everything to do with *setting up a blog*, but no! Also, I was using Wix at the time, so the post was completely irrelevant to me. Waste of time!

Sub-headings

Did I mention you need to break up the text? It isn't only images that can do that – sub-headings are pretty good too. The main purpose of a good sub-heading is to give sense of when there will be a small change of direction in the writing.

Like in this book, although right now I am discussing the umbrella term of how to write good content, I have broken in down into steps – so it is not one giant prose.

Media

This is so important to break up the text (and also to add in some colour to the mix). Good images can really compliment a post well. I hate reading a post and seeing picture that are unrelated to the text – like a picture of business people in a post about awesome new trainers, or a car in a post about how to deal with problems in your relationship!

What too many bloggers tend to forget is to fill in the 'Alt Text' and image description! Search engines (Google etc.) can't read images, so they don't know what writing is on your image. You need to provide an 'Alt Tag' to give the search engine an idea of what the image is about. Use *keywords* in your alt-tags.

Bullet Points / Number lists

Ok, so this one isn't used in all great posts, but it is still a very nice way to add some differentiation in your text (that's definitely the teacher in me talking)! You must admit that it is quite refreshing after reading half way down the post to get a nice, clear list of bullet points that simplify things even more.

Conclusion

Although you might not like to hear this, many readers tend to skim over a post and might therefore miss some crucial elements of the post. A conclusion can draw them back to the main points and lead them to re-read parts of the text again. They might even re-see the subscribe box and give you their email address.

Remember:

Your posts don't JUST have to be written! You can also deliver your posts in these ways:

- YouTube Videos

- Infographics

- Podcasts

- eBooks (mix individual existing posts to create
- an eBook)

- eCourse

- Presentations or Prezi's – lesson or an intro to a course etc.

Sharing buttons

This may seem obvious, but don't forget to add some sharing buttons to the bottom of every post. Your reader doesn't want to have to go up to the URL, copy it and then find the other page they want to paste it into! If you include these buttons, you are providing yet another service that makes your readers lives a bit easier. This also makes it more likely for your posts to get shared. Two birds with one very simple stone.

Content Upgrades

Content Upgrades are an awesome new way to (lets face it) "bribe" people to hand over their email addresses and subscribe to your mailing list. It is basically just bonus content for the post they have just read. It relates directly to what the reader has just read – rather than being a whole-site lead magnet.

It can be anything from a checklist or a worksheet, to the second half of a blog post. You can use many of the same things as your opt-in incentive for your content upgrade:

- Printables & Downloads

- Digital Workbook

- 2nd half of a blog post

- eCourse / Email Workshop (with downloadable worksheets and/or printables)

- Video / Audio download

- Downloadable cheat sheet / checklists

Brainstorm content ideas

When first starting out with your blog, it can be difficult to come up with a ton of post ideas in a hurry. This is why you should brainstorm ideas before you actually even launch your blog. Get the ideas in place so that you can just enjoy the writing process when you are due to publish a new post. I have my own brainstorm written out: A list of the categories on my website blog, which link on to another list of the sub-categories within them. You then write all the ideas you can think of to write about for each sub-category. You can create loads of strings from just one category!

For example, in my current brainstorm, under "Travel", I have a post idea about flying with a baby/toddler. I have then broken this down into more sub-sections: surviving long-haul flights, what to pack for the flight, what new toys/books I bought for our trip, best airlines to fly with a baby, most comfy airlines to use when with a baby etc. Doing things like this and really breaking down your ideas creates a huge amount of possible writing topics! Give it a go and see what I'm talking about. You might surprise yourself and think of topics that you never would have even thought to write about before.

Post Image Covers

One of the most useful tools that I use in my blogging life is an online image editing software called 'Canva'. Another one I used to use, which is very similar to it, is called, 'Crello'. These websites allow you to create blog post title pages for all different types of social media platforms – from YouTube banners to Pinterest images and blog post title pages.

You should always create around 2-3 different Pinterest images for each individual post you write (if you use Pinterest – which I assume you do, because you're smart!), but still stick to your branding style, so people still link it back to you. For example, if your brand colours are pink and purple, use these colours in your title covers, or if you use a certain font or style of writing / tone, make sure this is clear in too – people's minds will remember another post with the same branding and eventually, your blog will be imprinted in their brains every time they see those colours on Pinterest or other social networks.

Tip:

I use "Unsplash" and 'Death to the Stock Photo' to get my free images for blog post title covers etc. They provide completely free – and very professional stock photos for you to use in any way you wish. They only ask for you to credit the photographer. There are also other free websites to get images from too (Free Foto, Imagebase, Stock Free Images and many more).

Search Engine Optimisation

SEO is the way in which you optimise your website so that it ranks well in organic (natural) searches from search engines like Google. It is the methods, techniques and wording that you use to drive visitors to your blog. There are so many essential things we don't think about when writing our posts. These things could radically improve – or worsen your SEO ranking.

☺ **ONGOING ACTIVITY:**

Every time you write a post,
make sure you think about all of the below
points!

- Using a focus keyword enough

- Making sure the keyword is in the title of the post

- Adding a meta description (a summary of the content)

- Adding 'Alt attributes' to ALL images on our website (alternative text for when an image can't be displayed for some reason)

- The word count of the post itself (posts with over 1500 words do better)

- Including inbound *and* outbound links in every post

- Ensuring the links have a 'nofollow' tag (a way to tell search engines not to include your link in their visit count to the other website)

- Trying not to link a post text to another page with the same keyword

- SEO title length

This is where Yoast SEO comes in...

I love Yoast SEO!

This plugin gives you the ability to keep track of all of the above, and more, just by notifying you WHILE you actually write the post. It's awesome! Not only does Yoast warn you and teach you about your SEO status, but it also helps you to ensure that the readability of your post is at the optimum level. Yoast uses the 'Flesch Reading Ease' test to judge whether your post is easy to read. It tells you when you have repeated the start of sentences with the same word and how well you are using your subheadings and sentence length.

If you can use Yoast, or a plugin like it, you are sorted! If not, try to use my list above to help you ensure you are doing all you can with the SEO side of things to get your website visits as high as possible.

5

BE CONNECTED

Social Media: Create a following

I can definitely say that I've had a lot of painful pushing of posts to get more traffic and more subscribers to my blog! It finally happened, but it took a month of hard work and consistency. This is because I did it all backwards! I published the blog-site and then promoted like hell to get my brand heard…hard work is an understatement! If I had pre-promoted it, I would have already had a following and wouldn't be sitting here worrying about why nobody was subscribing.

You should start sharing the excitement of your "launch" on your social networking accounts at least a few weeks to a month before you launch your blog. This prepares people for something new and exciting, and it keeps them on their toes! The main social networking sites that bloggers tend to use are Pinterest, Twitter, Facebook, Instagram, LinkedIn and Google+ (although, I haven't yet got myself onto the last one). Think carefully about which platforms you want to use for social networking and spreading the word of your blog.

Many new bloggers jump straight into using all (or most) of the social networking sites, only to realise after a few weeks that their blog is spreading in completely different ways than they originally thought. They end up ditching one or two accounts and just focus on the ones that are bringing them traffic.

Schedule Pinterest

Pinterest is the number one social media site for many bloggers – including myself. It is often where the most views come from and where the loyalty of readers to your blog also begins. In order to keep your posts relevant and in the top feeds on Pinterest, it is extremely important to get a good schedule set up. At first, when I had only a few boards and about 10 posts, I would just set them up myself and keep a written schedule on Google Sheets for me to refer back to when sharing to group boards (you have to make sure you keep to the group board rules). After I started to grow my Pinterest following and engagement, had written a few more blog posts, and was joining more group boards, it was clear that to keep up with the schedule, I would need some help. Scheduling your own Pinterest pins is an absolute nightmare!! Especially when you realise that you have to share other posters pins too.

I started using an online Pinterest Pin scheduler called Tailwind! There are others, like 'BoardBooster' (which I may start using soon, for it's looping ability). It might cost a little, but it is SO worth it! Tailwind also has something called "Tailwind Tribes". These are user boards (some small, some gigantic!). You can share your post on these tribes to get post impressions out to millions of viewers!

Network with other bloggers in your niche

Get to know other bloggers in your "niche" (I use the word "niche" lightly). Believe it or not, in the *social* networking world, you actually have to be *social!* To show your support and appreciation towards others, you should share posts and comment on other influential (and even new) bloggers posts. Try to engage as much as possible on social networking, emails, courses, e-book downloads, general comments, questions, guest posts etc.

If you build a connection with a blogger before the launch of your blog, they may even help you promote it by commenting or sharing – or even mentioning you in one of their own posts! You could learn a lot just by following and speaking to a more experienced blogger. I know I have.

Guest Posts

One of the best ways to get to know other bloggers is to get them to guest post on your blog and for you to guest post on theirs. The first post I ever did was with a blog that I thought was great, but if I'm honest, I felt like the blogger had way too many ads on her site. The ads were unrelated to her content and it just looked a bit too...pushy! I actually turned down the second and third offers that I had!

This is because I had started to really think about what I want to be known for and whom I want to be associated with. There was no point in me posting on a blog, which was all about politics in other countries or all about fashion and makeup. Ok, I have blogged about makeup in the past, but that is not my specific niche and the readers of *that* blog would probably not find *my* blog very interesting, as it is unrelated to their needs.

The fourth guest post I was offered was by the marvellous *Marlee* from '*Dishes By Hand*'. She was very friendly, genuine and hard working! Her blog was closely linked to mine – but in a very different tone, but it worked! I posted on her blog and she posted on mine. Our posts both complimented each other's blogs perfectly, and we have stayed in contact since. I will promote her posts from time to time and she will also return the favour. Know your worth in whatever you do and whomever you work with and NEVER undersell yourself!

Facebook groups

I only stumbled across these little beauties towards the end of my first month blogging! Not only did sharing one post in a "normal" Facebook group managed to land me a Digital Media volunteer position at a single parent charity, but it also grew the traffic to my blog a LOT! I got my favourite early testimonial from a normal closed group about parenting. Even better than this...there are Facebook *"Pinterest Blogger Communities"*! These are amazing – people openly invite you to their Pinterest boards, and you can even start your own board and invite people from there.

The groups with the biggest following will likely give you more impressions, but be careful not to join just any group board. A group for ALL bloggers is unlikely to give you as many clicks as a group board that fits into your target audience. It is a great idea to start joining these boards before you launch, so you can stick them in your Tailwind schedule when you *are* ready to launch. It will also give you another way to promote your upcoming, amazing blog!

Email Marketing

How do you intend to grow your subscribers? What about communicating with them? Are you going to write all of their individual email addresses down and CC them all into an email you made? No, of course not. That would be CRAZY! You need an email-marketing platform to link your subscriptions to and to make communication with your subscribers easier. Email-marketing platforms that seem to be pretty popular at the moment include MailChimp, Convert Kit and Constant Contact.

As of July 2018:

ConvertKit

Starting at £21.98 ($29) / month with 30-day refund policy

Constant Contact

60 day free trial. Then starting at £15.16 ($20) / month

MailChimp

Free for up to 12,000 emails and 2000 subscribers. Then starting at £7.58 ($10) / month

For my blog (lifeitornot.com) I use MailChimp. This was initially because of the enticing free start-up costs. It also links with WordPress easily, although there are features that don't work as well as I would like. For this reason, although their interface is easy to use, and it's FREE, I am currently thinking about transferring my list to another platform – likely to be ConvertKit.

My reason for choosing ConvertKit (even with their high monthly payments) is simple. My main requirement at the moment is to add content upgrades in an easier way than I already do – without the need for a separate email delivery service provider.

Communicating with your subscribers

- How will you keep your subscribers coming back to your blog?

- Do you have anything interesting going on in your life? Any new products or courses to promote?

- Trending posts or guest posts that you want to share?

Three of the main ways that a blogger communicates with and stays in touch with their subscribers is via a newsletter, an RSS feed (for updates of each post you publish) and freebies. Consider sending a monthly or bi-monthly (twice a month) newsletter to your subscribers.

Although it is not a necessity, I personally think that a customized signature at the end of an email makes the sender look so much more professional and trusting! This signature should include your name, blog name, URL, logo, tagline (if you have one) and social buttons.

☺ ONGOING ACTIVITY:

Here is a list of things you could include in your newsletters...

- Trending post

- A bit about what you have been up to (*obviously, only include the relevant stuff – they don't want to know that you went shopping last Thursday!*)

- Promo for any new products, courses or eBooks etc.
- Exciting upcoming posts (*related to a personal or public holiday or event*)

- Guest posts

- Promo of another blogger (*it is always good to be a team player*)

- Coupons or promos from your affiliate programs

- Freebies

- Life-hacks

- Inspirational content

6

MONETISE YOUR BLOG

Almost every blogger wants to make money from their blog! But, what are the odds of you actually making a decent amount? First things first...you need traffic! How can you expect to make money if you don't have anyone visiting your blog in the first place? A good thing to remember is that (on average) less than 1 in every 100 visitors to your blog will actually click on a link or an ad – let alone *buy* what you are promoting.

If we are being realistic, in order to make any decent amount of money, you need at least 5k unique visitors every month. This is not a steadfast rule; it is just the general number that seems to be the standard for making a good amount of money.

- Lets say you have a few affiliate links to products that, if bought through your link, would give you £10 each.

- If you then have 1000 unique visitors to your blog in one month and 10 of them click on a link **AND** buy the product, you will have earned yourself £100.

- Now lets look at it as if you are linking to bigger-money products that would give you around £40 each sale.

- If you had the same numbers as above (1k visitors with 10 clicking and buying), you would have made £400 in that month.

There *are* bloggers who have made much more than that in their first few months, but it is rare. This does not mean to say that you CAN'T make *some* money in the beginning though. There are various monetisation strategies that you can use to start bringing money in…it just all gets a bit easier with a good following and traffic.

Google AdSense

I was a late starter to Google AdSense, because of all the problems I had using it on my Wix website! Once I had it all set up on WordPress, I earned 25p in just a few days...not bad for a completely new blogger, eh? Well, I was chuffed anyway! Google AdSense is a free monetization system. You allow Google to place ads on your website and you get paid in a variety of ways. The main ways are:

1. **Cost Per Thousand Impressions – CPM**
   Every time the page the ad is on is loaded and at least 50% of the ad is displayed for at least 1 second

2. **Cost Per Engagement – CPE**
   Every time the ad is engaged with (hovered over, clicked etc.)

3. **Cost Per Click – CPC**
   Every time the ad is clicked

One of the things that prevented me from using AdSense Ads straight away was that I didn't just want any old ads on my blog. I didn't want my readers to be put off – I want my readers to enjoy their time on my blog! What I didn't know at the time is that AdSense actually allows you to block certain types of ads from your website! Yay! So, I started blocking those annoying ads about finance and cars that are *completely* unrelated to parenting or personal growth, and I started allowing **only** things that I thought my readers would need or want.

Become an Affiliate Partner

What is an Affiliate?

Affiliate marketing is basically performance-based marketing. A business allows you to call yourself an "affiliate partner" while you promote their products or services. They then reward (pay) you for each customer that buys something from their website if it is bought from one of your affiliate links. An affiliate link is just a special URL that is created using your special affiliate ID (created when you sign up to the company).

For example, if you are an Amazon affiliate:

➤ You put an affiliate link to a recipe book into one of your posts

➤ Someone clicks on that link and buys the product (or a different product on that page)

➤ You get paid a percentage of that product's cost

Shweet!!

Find affiliate programs

Of course, nobody is really going to sign you up to their affiliate program if you don't even have a live blog website yet, but it never hurts to be prepared. Create a list of around 10 potential affiliate programs that you would like to be associated with when your blog site goes live. Remember to only look at businesses and networks that actually relate to your blog! If you write about making money, your readers are not going to want ads all over the place for buying a flash new car or baby stuff. It helps if you also have a small paragraph outlining what your blog is about.

Most programs ask for a short explanation about your blog and how you will use it to benefit their program and vice versa. If you write a convincing statement and have a decent flow of traffic to your site, you are more likely to be accepted – or even *invited* into an affiliate program!

How to use affiliate links

The main way that an affiliate link is used is by putting it into a text link in a post. It might be linked to something the author is suggesting the reader should use, or it could be something that you actually use! Write a post or a review, don't just spurt random ads for your affiliate sales! I recently wrote a review post about SiteGround because they really have been amazing for me since I started using them as my host. They deserve a pat on the back and more customers – so why not put an affiliate link in there for myself while I'm at it?

You don't only have to use in-text links. Most businesses provide options for just text, just image, text and image and banners. Personally, I'm not a fan of banners. I think they take a lot away from the personalisation of your website and make it seem too spammy! Many businesses also offer special promotions or offers. Boots regularly send out updates on their deals, and other affiliate programs send out coupon codes etc.

Sponsored Posts / Product Reviews

A sponsored post is when you get paid to publish a post on your blog. The advertiser might ask you to write a post about their business in order to promote that business, or they might even write the post themselves. Sponsored posts can cost the advertiser (and earn you) between £300 - £1500 on average, depending on blog traffic and reader retention etc.

A Product Review post is when you review a product and then (usually) get to keep the product. Although it's not exactly monetising your blog, because you don't always get "paid" for it. You are still doing a worthwhile exchange (providing you don't undersell yourself) – a blog post for a product or service!

Selling your own products or services

There are probably a few things that you either do, or provide for your readers that you could sell for actual money! The main things that bloggers create and sell are eCourses and eBooks, with freelance writing services following closely behind. Are you a consultant on a specific topic? Or do you offer a specific service? If so, you should make these clear on your website and make an obvious 'Call to Action' for your readers. Give them an incentive – maybe provide them with a freebie to entice them and make them want your product or service. For example, with this book I provided a free chapter to new subscribers – with a link to the download URL. If they like the chapter, they might go on and actually buy a copy of the full eBook! Obviously, this was promoted heavily beforehand on social media and the offer of the freebie was also included in pop-up posts and subscription boxes all over my website.

Disclosures

Whenever you receive compensation for something (whether it be a free product or payment in money), you have to disclose it to your readers. A disclosure shows your readers that you are honest and trustworthy, and it also protects the advertiser.

This disclosure has to be somewhere obvious – it can't just be one little notice on your homepage, as most readers won't even click on your homepage to be able to see it at all. You should ideally have a whole separate page for your disclosure and each individual post that features an affiliate link, sponsored or review post or advertising should have a short sentence explaining that you are an affiliate or are receiving compensation in some way. You can then link this smaller disclosure to the separate page. The smaller disclosure (on post pages etc.) does not have to be screaming at the reader in giant bold letters, it can just be added in a "passing" way.

For example, rather than writing, "This post has an affiliate link. Please click HERE for more info", you could just include the link and then write (affiliate link) after the link text. The writing in brackets should be a link to the disclosure page.

Media Kit

You may have seen quite a few influential bloggers offering a media kit to advertisers and businesses. You may have also thought once or twice that you are nowhere near popular enough to even *need* a media kit?

Wrong!

If you want to work with brands – at any stage of your blog journey, you need a media kit. A media kit is basically a document (normally a .PDF) which potential advertisers, businesses or brands can download or request in order to learn more about you before they request a collaboration.

<u>Your media kit should include</u>:

- A short biography about you and your blog

- Testimonials

- Statistics – Subscribers, monthly visits, followers on social media etc.

  If you are just starting out, don't think that you can't still include some of your stats. You might only have 10 subscribers, but you probably have over 150 daily page views, right? Work that out over a month and it's about 4500 monthly page views. Rather than putting your website page views, you could write that you have over 100k monthly Pinterest views etc. Get the point? You are still being honest, but just bigging-up your best numbers.

- Images – professional ones!

- Previous work you have collaborated with (if any). If you haven't worked with any brands yet, you can include whom you are an affiliate partner with.

- How you want to collaborate – ads, sponsored posts, social media, product reviews, giveaways or promotions etc.

- Contact details – they need to be able to contact you

7

THE NITTY-GRITTY

Hidden costs of setting up a blog

Nothing good comes for free!

I have included my start-up costs here for you to get an idea of what I (very unexpectedly) spent in just the first two months of setting up and launching my blog.

This would work out at about £23.40 monthly – for all of it altogether. Not actually that bad when you think about it! I probably didn't *NEED* to pay for a Premium WordPress theme, or Tailwind, but they have both proven to be more than worth it!

PRODUCT	PRICE
Wix Premium Website / Domain (for 1 year)	£46.56
SiteGround hosting (for 1 year). After the first year, this increases to £90.48	£54.12
WordPress Premium Theme (one-off payment)	£42.27
Domain transfer	£11.32
Tailwind (for 1 year. I got a deal that day)	£90.46
Official 'Wix' created logo	£9.03
"The Million Dollar Blog" by Natasha Courtenay-Smith	£13.99
"The Digital Business Start-Up Workbook" by Cheryl Rickman	£12.99
TOTAL	£280.74 ($370.37)

If I had gone straight to WordPress, rather than mucking around with Wix, it would have been £222.86 and I could have saved £57.88!

Favicon

A favicon is that little image you can see on the individual tabs on your browser. Check it out now and notice how all the different websites you are on have its own little image! The favicon not only makes your website look much more professional, but it also links everything back to your blog. It is a gentle reminder of your logo and brand. A favicon is VERY easy to set up.

To find out how to do it with your particular host, just Google it and the method should come up straight away. With WordPress.org, all you need to do is go to:

Admin – Appearance – Customise - Site Identity – Image, and then upload your logo.

Job done.

Google Analytics Tracking

Google Analytics was my constant source of happiness and misery when I first started my blog. One day it would show 400 visits to the blog and the next it would show only 20…I would freak out! Now, I know better.

No longer do I twiddle my fingers with delight (or worry) 5 times a day to see any changes. These days, I still look at my Google Analytics once every morning. This is not *just* to see how the traffic is doing though. It is also a great way to determine how my posts are doing on each social network, and organically (through a natural Google or browser search). Through analysing my Google Analytics tracking, I can decide how and where I need to push posts and pins. I can see which social media platforms are driving the most traffic, which posts are doing well (or not so well) and even what the demographics of my readers are! Amazing!

If I look right now, I can tell you that currently, 93% of my readers are female, aged 25-34. Great! That's my target demographic. I can also tell you that the top five countries of my readers this month are 49% from the US, 22% from the UK, 10% from Canada, 5% from Australia and 2% from India.

EPILOGUE

Be prepared to influence, inspire and make a difference

Although I know I want to influence and inspire other women – especially mum's, I never thought that I could start doing it in just the first two weeks of launching my blog!

I shared one of my new posts about overcoming the struggle of being a new single mum to a single parent support group on Facebook, and the next thing you know, I've started a thread about the post and I was asked to work with the organization as a 'Social Media Volunteer' for their Single Parents Support Charity. I have since joined their action in contacting my local MP to get an answer to the misconceptions about the rules surrounding single parenting and taking a child abroad. The many comments I have received on social media about how much my readers enjoy reading my posts and how useful they are to them is just heart-warming. I know I will do my readers proud – just as they do me proud every time they tell me that they used my advice and it worked for them!

I hope this book has been informative and has helped you to make a plan of action before you step into the giant world of the Blogosphere! Don't be afraid to get things wrong – God only knows how many mistakes I made in my first month!

But…

I also did a ton of things right and now the results are showing! You will have the same ups and downs and you might even take off to be the next big   thing   in   the   Blogosphere!

ABOUT THE AUTHOR

Sarah Leigh

Founder of 'Life It Or Not'
Lifestyle, Personal Growth and Parenting Blog

Empowering Women to Become Their Own Inspiration

Sarah Leigh is a 30-year old single mum who lives in East London with her 1-year-old daughter. She is the founder of Life It Or Not – a Parenting and Lifestyle blog all about helping other women (especially mums) to become empowered and self-inspired!

Her own inspiration to do this comes from her own life struggles with leaving home at 16, living with

Cardiomyopathy and Heart Failure, a partially deaf daughter, a Cancer scare, single parenthood and much more. Sarah is an influencer in her field because she has single-handedly turned her negatives into positives and now leads a wonderful life, full of fun, travel, inner-peace and love.

Contact me:

Website:
www.lifeitornot.com

Facebook:
www.facebook.com/lifeitornot

Pinterest:
www.pinterest.com/lifeitornot

Twitter:
www.twitter.com/lifeitornotblog

Instagram:
www.instagram.com/lifeitornot_blog

Linked In:
www.linkedin.com/in/lifeitornot

Email:
lifeitornot1@gmail.com

Disclaimer

Although the author has made every effort to ensure that the information in this book was correct at press time, the author does not assume and hereby disclaim any liability to any part for any loss, damage, or disruption caused by errors or omissions, whether such errors or omissions result from negligence, accident, or any other cause.